Facts About the Cicada

By Lisa Strattin

© 2021 Lisa Strattin

FREE BOOK

FREE FOR ALL SUBSCRIBERS

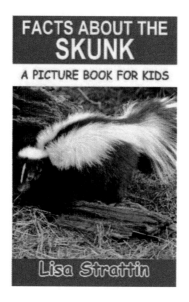

LisaStrattin.com/Subscribe-Here

BOX SET

- **FACTS ABOUT THE POISON DART FROGS**
- **FACTS ABOUT THE THREE TOED SLOTH**
- **FACTS ABOUT THE RED PANDA**
- **FACTS ABOUT THE SEAHORSE**
- **FACTS ABOUT THE PLATYPUS**
- **FACTS ABOUT THE REINDEER**
- **FACTS ABOUT THE PANTHER**
- **FACTS ABOUT THE SIBERIAN HUSKY**

LisaStrattin.com/BookBundle

Facts for Kids Picture Books by Lisa Strattin

Little Blue Penguin, Vol 92

Chipmunk, Vol 5

Frilled Lizard, Vol 39

Blue and Gold Macaw, Vol 13

Poison Dart Frogs, Vol 50

Blue Tarantula, Vol 115

African Elephants, Vol 8

Amur Leopard, Vol 89

Sabre Tooth Tiger, Vol 167

Baboon, Vol 174

Sign Up for New Release Emails Here

LisaStrattin.com/subscribe-here

All information in this book has been carefully researched and checked for factual accuracy. However, the author and publisher makes no warranty, express or implied, that the information contained herein is appropriate for every individual, situation or purpose and assume no responsibility for errors or omissions. The reader assumes the risk and full responsibility for all actions, and the author will not be held responsible for any loss or damage, whether consequential, incidental, special or otherwise, that may result from the information presented in this book.

All images are free for use or purchased from stock photo sites or royalty free for commercial use.

Some coloring pages might be of the general species due to lack of available images.

I have relied on my own observations as well as many different sources for this book and I have done my best to check facts and give credit where it is due. In the event that any material is used without proper permission, please contact me so that the oversight can be corrected.

COVER IMAGE

https://flickr.com/photos/derekmarkham/3881168931

ADDITIONAL IMAGES

https://flickr.com/photos/132295270@N07/42466517075

https://flickr.com/photos/tone-red/3135378566

https://flickr.com/photos/132295270@N07/48368768366

https://flickr.com/photos/eroc/4868292529

https://flickr.com/photos/amboo213/3614038415

https://flickr.com/photos/polunsky/5775738723

https://flickr.com/photos/23099933@N03/13967430312

https://flickr.com/photos/wonderferret/95714464

https://flickr.com/photos/elisfanclub/367713289

https://flickr.com/photos/sidm/49839820393

Contents

INTRODUCTION

Cicadas are winged insects that appear every summer, sometimes after *years* of living underground. Cicadas live underground most of their life as larvae (immature insects) and nymphs, and some stay there for years before they come to the surface for a short time. After they emerge to the surface and reach maturity, they make a buzzing sound that is their mating call.

They spend a short amount of time above ground where they mate and then the females lay their eggs. When the eggs hatch, the larvae fall to the ground and burrow underground where they will stay until they mature. Cicadas have very thin, transparent wings that can appear to be rainbow colored in the sun.

CHARACTERISTICS

There are about 3,000 different species of cicadas known around the world. There are two major classifications of cicadas: annuals and periodicals. Most annuals come to the surface yearly while periodicals come to the surface every 13 to 17 years.

Most of the male cicadas sing; they sing to attract a mate and when they sense danger. Males and females both make sounds by clicking their wings. Some of the cicada's songs can be heard from over a mile away! Each different species of cicada has their own individual type of song.

Cicadas do not sting or bite, so they are not harmful to anyone or anything.

APPEARANCE

Cicadas come in a few different colors; their bodies can be green, black, and brown and their eyes can be red, white, or blue. The top part of their body is a dark color while the underside is a lighter color.

Adult cicadas will vary in color depending on their species, but they all have big eyes that bulge out from their head. Their oval shaped wings are transparent and have veins in them that sometimes look like a *W*.

LIFE STAGES

Cicadas are different from many other kinds of insects. After mating, the female will scratch holes into wood surfaces, like tree branches, and lay up to 20 eggs in each place. She may scratch 40 to 50 of these holes and lay up to 400 eggs!

Once the eggs hatch (usually within 6 to 10 weeks), the larvae will drop to the ground. Once they hit the ground, they will burrow into the ground where they will stay. To eat, the larvae (also called nymphs) will suck the liquid out of tree roots.

Once she lays the eggs, the mother cicada does not care for the babies, and they are left to fend for themselves.

LIFE SPAN

Cicadas can have a life span of 2 to 5 years for annuals and up to 17 years for periodicals. However, once they come above ground, they stay for less than a month before they die.

SIZE

Cicadas are a small insect. Depending on the species, they can range in size from 3/4 to 2 1/4 inches long. When they are eggs, the eggs are about the size of a grain of rice.

HABITAT

Adult cicadas normally live in and on trees, the crown, trunk, and twigs. They prefer deciduous trees rather than coniferous trees.

The nymph's habitat is underground where they feed off of the juices of roots from trees and plants.

DIET

Cicadas are herbivores and they do not have any teeth. Instead of teeth, cicada have a beak that they use to get liquid from tree and plant roots. The larvae suck juices from the roots of plants and trees while underground. Adult periodicals use their beak to suck the juices from trees and shrubs. Adult annual cicadas do not eat.

FRIENDS AND ENEMIES

Cicadas have many predators in the world. When the swarms emerge from underground, they are a snack for many different types of animals.

Birds, mites, fungal diseases, and cicada killers are some of the known predators. The cicada killer will use its venom to paralyze the cicadas and drag them to their burrows. They then lay their eggs in the cicadas and use them as food for their larvae.

Rodents, snakes, lizards, racoons, opossums, dogs, and cats will also eat cicadas.

SUITABILITY AS PETS

Cicadas have not been kept in captivity, so knowledge about them as pets is very sparse. Since cicadas live on a liquid diet from plants and roots, it would be difficult for someone to keep them as a pet. There have been other bugs in similar families who have been kept in captivity, but there is no evidence that these same methods would work for cicadas.

If one were to keep cicadas as pets, they would not be a very good pet since they have a short life span (about a month) above ground.

COLOR ME

COLOR ME

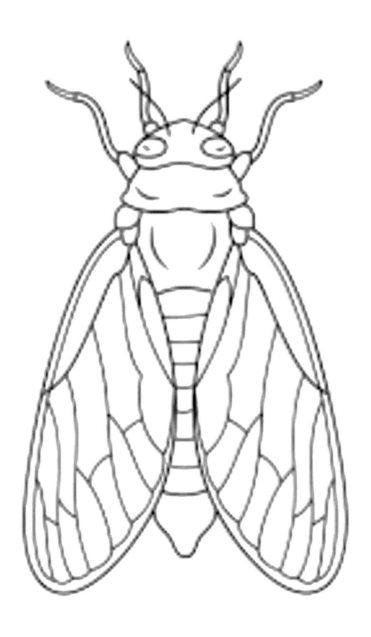

COLOR ME

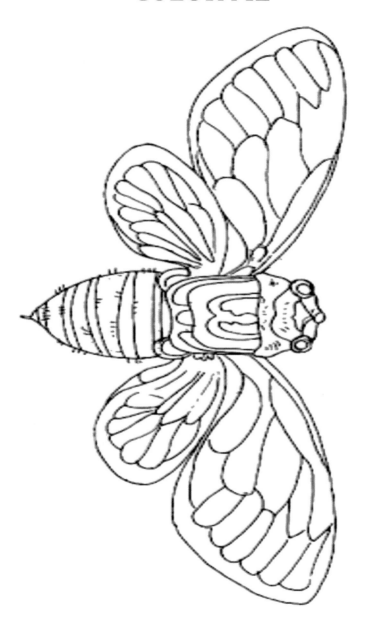

COLOR ME

COLOR ME

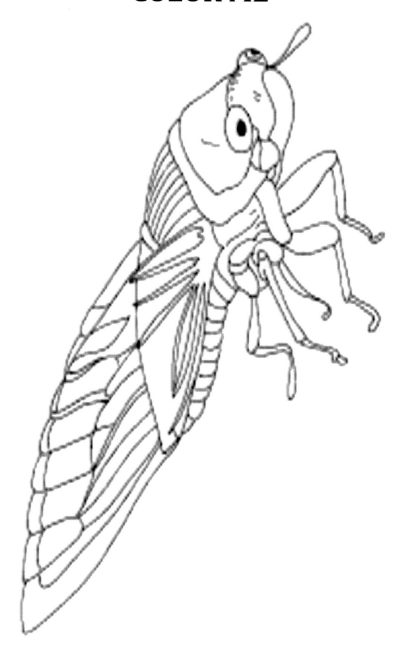

COLOR ME

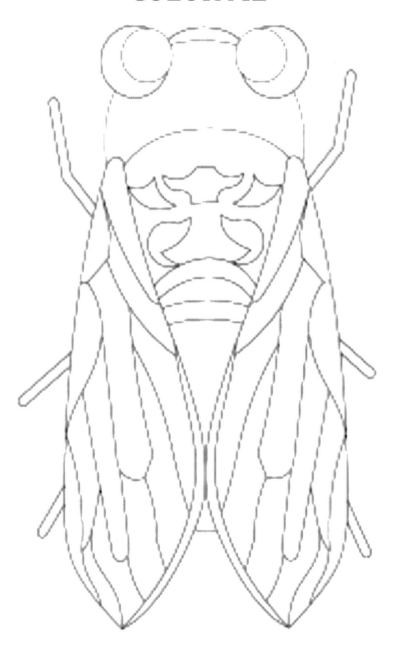

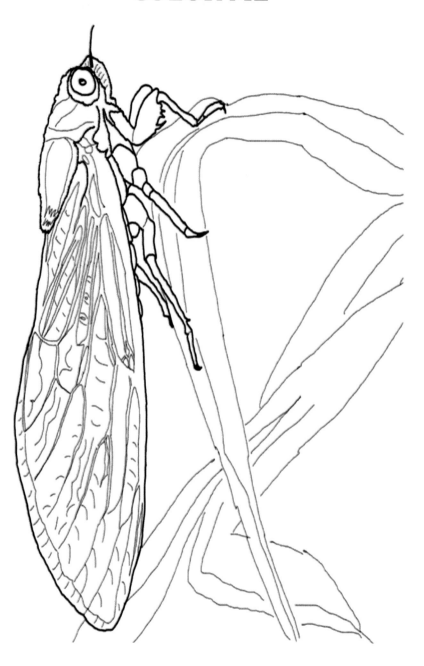

COLOR ME

Please leave me a review here:

LisaStrattin.com/Review-Vol-408

For more Kindle Downloads Visit Lisa Strattin Author Page on Amazon Author Central

amazon.com/author/lisastrattin

To see upcoming titles, visit my website at LisaStrattin.com– most books available on Kindle!

LisaStrattin.com

FREE BOOK

FOR ALL SUBSCRIBERS – SIGN UP NOW

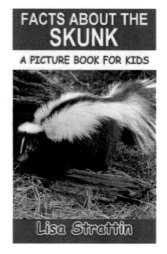

LisaStrattin.com/Subscribe-Here

LisaStrattin.com/Facebook

LisaStrattin.com/Youtube

Made in the USA
Las Vegas, NV
19 May 2021